A First-Start® Easy Reader

This easy reader contains only 64 different words, repeated often to help the young reader develop word recognition and interest in reading.

and	high	now	slide
are	I	off	steps
big	is	oh	swing
bucket	it	on	swings
but	jumps	opens	tall
climbs	ladder	opposite	the
closes	like	opposites	they
do	likes	over	things
down	little	play	through
empty	look	playground	to
full	loud	pulls	too
games	low	pushes	together
gate	Lucy	quiet	tunnel
go	Luke	sad	twins
goes	Luke's	same	under
happy	no	short	up

I Like Opposites

by Joanne Mattern
illustrated by Jerry Smath

Luke and Lucy are twins.
They look the same.

But they like to do opposite things!

Luke and Lucy go to the playground.

Luke OPENS the playground gate.

Lucy CLOSES the playground gate.

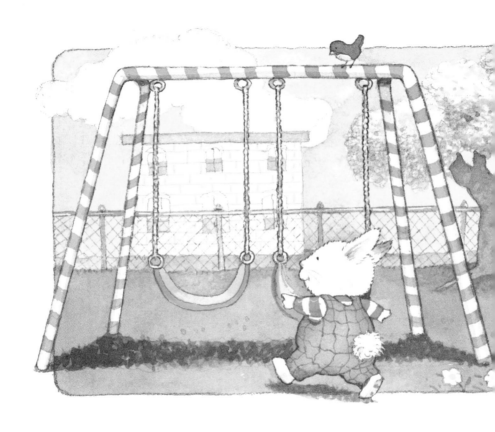

Luke goes on the BIG swing.

Lucy goes on the LITTLE swing.

Luke swings HIGH.

Lucy swings LOW.

Luke climbs the SHORT ladder.

Lucy climbs the TALL ladder.

Luke goes DOWN the slide.

But Lucy goes UP the slide!

Luke jumps ON the steps.

Lucy jumps OFF the steps.

Luke goes UNDER the tunnel.

Lucy goes OVER the tunnel.

Luke PUSHES Lucy through
the tunnel.

Lucy PULLS Luke through the tunnel.

Luke likes to play LOUD games.

Lucy likes to play QUIET games.

Luke's bucket is FULL.

But now it is EMPTY!

Oh, no! Luke is SAD.

Lucy is sad too!

Now Lucy and Luke are HAPPY.

Luke and Lucy like
to do opposite things.

But they like to play together!